Customer Loyalty 101

How to Grow Your Circle of Loyal Customers and Why
the Millions of $$$ in Customer Service and
Phone Skills Training Haven't Worked

By Jackie Morey

www.JackieMorey.com

This book is INTERACTIVE – to get your
FREE training videos, access to more resources,
and updates, please click on the link above.

Dedication

To my Mom and Dad who first taught me all three Keys, especially Key #1. You have both inspired me to reach for my dreams, to read voraciously and to write for the purpose of leaving a legacy.

To my handsome, faithful, trustworthy and godly Husband who's my #1 Fan and whom I'm his #1 Fan. You are a man of high integrity and I'm so grateful for you. You are the one who encouraged me to begin this journey, you supported me throughout, and you motivated me during the toughest moments to finish this book and then to go achieve so much more. I deeply love you.

To our children – Michael and Alyssa. You are both the main "Whys" that I wrote this book. During the nights when I was exhausted…while you both slept in your rooms, thinking about you years down the road – carried me through the "messy middle" so that I could complete this book and leave a legacy for you. May you learn these principles and use them with pure motives, to truly serve and love God and love others.

To my brothers and sisters, nephews and nieces. May you reach for the highest goals ordained by God.

To my friends near and far who have encouraged, supported, "hung out" with me, and prayed for our family through all these years…thank you very, very much.

To all my Customers, may you reach greater levels of success and fulfillment in your businesses and your personal life – as you embrace and apply the principles and strategies in this book. Richest blessings to you.

Now onward and upward!

Customer Strategy Academy, LLC
16212 Bothell-Everett Hwy
Suite F111
Mill Creek, WA. 98012
Email: CustomerStrategyAcademy@Gmail.com

Limits of Liability and Disclaimer of Warranty
The author and publisher shall not be liable for your misuse of this material. This book is for strictly informational and educational purposes.

Disclaimer
The views expressed are those of the author / webmaster and do not reflect the official policy or position of the publisher or Customer Strategy Academy, LLC.

This book is similar to "How To Stop Losing Patients NOW." But it caters more to companies and businesses that are not in the Healthcare Industry.

Copyright Use and Public Information
Unless otherwise noted, images have been used with public information laws.

Table of Contents

"Customers, Clients or Patients are LOYAL because they perceive that whatever they receive from you in product, service and overall Customer Experience is at least DOUBLE if not more, than the price they pay."

~Jackie Morey

Introduction

 Hi, I'm Jackie Morey. Welcome to "Customer Loyalty 101.

Have you or your company, small business, professional practice, department or team spent hundreds of $$$ on Customer Service or Phone Skills training, and yet you've **still** lost customers to your competitors on a regular basis?

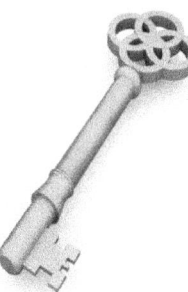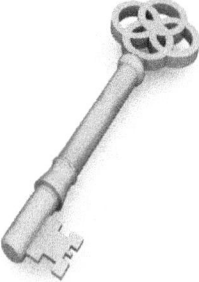

You are about to discover 3 Lost KEYS that your company must acquire and use to your advantage – in order to develop Customer Loyalty in a world <u>where your clients can comparison shop as well as permanently damage your reputation online in seconds</u> on their mobile device.

Who Is This For?

If you are in business as an Entrepreneur, Legal, Financial, or Accounting Professional, a small to medium business Owner, a Manager, Supervisor or someone who interacts directly with customers **and**…

- You're tired of losing valuable clients, and have had enough of customers leaving your company or practice

- You've had enough of the gut-wrenching stress and dejection every time customers post negative online reviews

- You want to stop your online reputation from further being damaged

- You want to halt the trend of finding out that your angry or merely satisfied customers are flocking to your competitors

- You'd like to significantly boost your revenue

- You want to thrive and **not** just survive in a challenging Economy

- You and your staff want to master the easiest and most effective way of taking care of angry or disgruntled customers

- You'd like to build rapport, connect more meaningfully with your customers, and tap into the most powerful marketing strategy in the world which is word-of-mouth advertising, then this book is **just** for you.

This Is Your Opportunity to Stand Out Amidst the Status Quo and the Mediocre

Research shows that businesses who provide **poor** customer service will not only lose sales, but invariably also lose their customers to competitors.

Oh, no…you don't **ever** want to lose your good customers to your competitors, do you?

Research also shows that it's costing businesses an average of **$289** per Lost Customer per year.

Multiply that one customer whose "average lifetime with the company" is hypothetically 5 years, and that's **$1,445** of lost revenue…for just that **one** customer.

If that same business loses 2 customers in one year, that's **$2,890** of squandered revenue.

And that's not even taking into account **all the referrals** that those customers could've sent their way. And **the referrals of those referrals**.

If you take into consideration **lost referrals** from a good customer for this customer's "average lifetime with the company", that could easily be worth another **$7,225**.

Can you see how lost revenue can rapidly and exponentially escalate?

Mind-blowing, isn't it?

And yet many companies still put a lot more emphasis on Advertising and Marketing, and very little into cultivating Customer Loyalty.

According to the American Express 2011 Global Customer Service Barometer, an annual report conducted by Echo Research in 10 nations.

- "Good customer service leads to repeat business"
- "Poor service leads to lost sales"
- "Consumers are *more* likely to tell others about their *poor* customer service experiences"
- "Consumers will switch brands to get better Customer Service"

And in the American Express 2012 Global Customer Service Barometer, here are their findings.

- "Consumers think businesses are paying less attention to providing good customer service."

- "Only 7% of consumers said that the customer service experiences they have with companies usually 'exceed their expectations' (compared to 6% in 2011) and 31% said that companies usually 'miss their expectations' for customer service (compared to 29% in 2011).

- "Most consumers still believe that companies are helpful, but aren't doing anything extra to keep their business."

- "Consumers will spend more with companies that provide excellent service."

- "Consumers value excellent service – some are willing to pay for it, while others expect it."

- "Consumers are telling more people about their customer service experiences."

- "On average, they tell 15 people about their good experiences (up from 9 in 2011), and 24 people about their bad experiences (up from 16 in 2011)."

- "When it comes to poor customer service experiences, 56% of consumers talk to people about them all the time."

- "Over 55% of consumers have intended to conduct a business transaction or make a purchase, <u>but decided not to</u>, based on a poor service experience."

- "More than a third of consumers (35%) have lost their temper with a customer service professional in the past year."

- 59% of consumers pointed out that the two (2) main issues most likely to influence them to switch brands or companies are 'a rude or unresponsive customer service representative' and also 'being shuffled from representative to representative with no resolution of their issue'.

So you see, it's really <u>your</u> window of opportunity to simply tweak some things, then shine, stand out and truly become world-class.

Words of Wisdom from Jeff Bezos

Founder and CEO of Amazon.com – Billionaire Jeff Bezos has this to say about word-of-mouth advertising,

> *"If you do build a great experience, customers tell each other about that. Word of mouth is very powerful."* –Jeff Bezos

You see, word-of-mouth advertising or Social Proof applies to any industry…yes, **even your industry**.

Have you ever been referred by a colleague, family member or friend, to a Doctor, a Dentist, a Financial Planner, a Real Estate Agent, an Accountant, an Attorney, a restaurant, or a must-see movie?

Ahhh, there you go… that's word-of-mouth advertising at work.

It's no big secret…people are more likely to trust the companies, professionals, and small businesses who have been referred to them by their friends, colleagues, relatives or neighbors – in other words, the people they already **know**, **like** and **trust**.

Wouldn't you like to be the one whom people recommend, when they ask for a Service Provider, Real Estate Professional, Financial Planner, Sales Executive, Attorney, or Accountant?

Of course, you would.

Then let's begin the journey of getting more and more word-of-mouth referrals!

Side Note: Can you guess how I found out about amazon.com? Yes, a friend told me all about it a while back, when all they were doing was selling used books!

There it is again…word-of-mouth.

As Jeff Bezos said, others giving you social proof is quite powerful.

Here's What We'll Talk About

I have **tons** of great information to share with you, but I didn't want to write a "War and Peace" novel.

One short book, though, isn't nearly enough time to share everything there is to know about Customer Loyalty, how to develop this in your company, and give you every single Key there is.

But I promise that before we're done, and you're ready for more, I'm going to show you how to get continuing education on this very important topic.

In a few moments, I'm going to hand over 3 Keys to you and some Actionable Ideas so that you can start using them today and move your clients to the top of the Customer Loyalty scale and keep them there.

I believe that the quicker you take action, the better your chances are for success.

Here's what we'll talk about.

First, we'll discuss The Definition of Customer Loyalty. What exactly **is it**?

We'll also discuss some of the Differences between Customer Satisfaction and Customer Loyalty – there are HUGE differences, it **is** a BIG deal, and I can hardly wait to show you why.

Next, I'll share with you 7 Compelling Benefits your Company will get when you focus on cultivating Customer Loyalty not merely Customer Satisfaction.

We could easily list 15 BIG benefits, but I'll briefly share seven (7).

Finally, I'll reveal 3 Lost Keys your company must have in your Backpack, and **use** to your advantage in order to develop and cultivate Customer Loyalty.

My Delicious Steakhouse Story…NOT!

J ust to whet your appetite, allow me to tell you a true story that happened to me.
I promise to give you four (4) Takeaways from this.

Oh, and by the way, let me make clear that the photo here is **not** a picture of the steaks we had that night. It's just a photo to make you hungry. ☺

Anyway, kidding aside, my Husband – Jim – and I had been working hard and we needed a break. So we decided to go on a mid-week date.

We were *really* looking forward to a relaxed steak dinner.

It was one of those steak franchises.

We were **satisfied** from previous visits to other locations. So we thought we'd try the one near our home.

It would be our first time there.

Well, things didn't turn out the way we expected.

It was a weeknight – the place wasn't very full.

"**Good**," we thought…we could get quick service.

We were promptly seated and began to look through the menu.

Wait a second.

There were no utensils or napkins on the table and our server failed to notice this as she seated us.

"Hmmm. Ok, no problem," we thought, "the server should be here **any moment** to bring some, and she could take our order."

Well, "**any moment**" turned out to be about **20 minutes**…in a nearly empty restaurant!

Uh-oh. This wasn't a good sign.

My Husband and I finally placed our order and we began talking about our busy day, our kiddos, and our upcoming vacation.

We were really hungry, and eagerly awaited our meals.

We waited and waited. After **35 minutes**, still no food! And no one bothered to let us know what was going on.

Pitiful!

Finally…at the **40-minute mark**, our meals arrived. Whew!

Jim's porter house steak was just fine, but there was a problem with my filet mignon.

Just for the record, my Husband likes rare. In his own words, he says, "I can eat something that's still moving."

As for me, I like mine medium well.

As I cut into my steak, I soon found out that it was **way** undercooked. It had lots of red, dripping from the center, it was practically "Moo-ing!"

Then after quite a while of my Husband trying, he finally got the server's attention and asked if she could take it back to have it cooked the way I had asked.

We know these things happen, right? No big deal.

So she took my plate to have it re-done.

In the meantime, Jim, the gentleman that he is, considerately stopped eating his steak, shared his veggies with me and we ate some more bread while we waited. And waited, and waited some more.

Finally, my meal came back and I dug in – really hungry now.

Whoa, what was **this**? My steak was now **way overcooked**!

(Note: This is not the actual photo of my steak that day. It looks pretty close, though.)

I mean there is "medium well", then there's "well done"…and then there's **"charcoal"**!

Oh my!

I hoped that I could find a piece of edible steak in my charcoal steak.

Sigh…

After a couple of minutes, I gave up. It was **burnt to a crisp**.

I was very disappointed, disgruntled, **and** by now, <u>ultra- hungry</u>.

Their Shocking Solution

After Jim finished his steak, the server came back and asked us how things were. We expressed our problem.

Now *here's the thing* – she didn't even offer to fix it.

She just went right into asking if we wanted dessert. Pitiful.

And she didn't even offer **that** dessert for free to somehow alleviate the problem.

Well, we didn't want to wait for dessert because we didn't know how long **that** would take.

So we politely declined, asked for our bill and we asked to talk to the manager.

After we paid, eventually the manager stopped by and asked what the problem was.

We explained what had happened.

After lamenting our unpleasant evening at her restaurant, we waited for her response.

What would she do? How would she handle this simple, easy-to-solve problem?

Her resolution was – *now get this* – to offer us a coupon for **half-off the 2ND entrée** at **our next visit** to that location!

Next visit?!

With the way she was handling this problem, did she actually think we would come back for a "**next visit**"?!

Was she serious? Apparently she was!

We were flabbergasted…Jim and I just stared at each other in utter amazement. It wasn't a joke – at least it wasn't *intended* as one.

Then she turned and left.

And we got up and left…**never ever** to return! Not even to any of the other locations of that franchise anywhere in our city.

Do you think I'd recommend this restaurant to any of our friends, relatives, neighbors, or colleagues?

Never.

I'm sure you can think of a similar story that happened to you.

No pun intended, but "Holy cow!" Does this really happen in this day and age, after hundreds of millions of $$$ have been spent on Customer Service training and everything else regarding Customers?

Unfortunately, the answer is a resounding yes!

> *Does this really happen in this day and age, after hundreds of millions of $$ have been spent on Customer Service training, and everything else regarding Customers?*
>
> *Unfortunately, the answer is a resounding yes!*

The Five-Part Obstacle Course They Used to Lose Us, As Their Customers

L et's give the steakhouse the benefit of the doubt and say that they may honestly not have wanted this to happen to us.
But what gives?

Obstacle #1 – The server didn't take our orders promptly. She gave us menus as soon as she seated us, but didn't come back to see what we had decided on, until 20 minutes later! And this happened in a nearly empty restaurant. **Unacceptable**.

Obstacle #2 – I ordered my filet mignon "Medium Well." The chef undercooked my steak so much so that it was dripping with lots of blood. And then, when given a chance to do it right, the chef charcoal-burnt my dinner! **Pitiful**.

Obstacle #3 – The server didn't apologize for my burnt-to-the-crisp charcoal steak. She didn't seem to care how hungry I still was. **Awful**.

Obstacle #4 – The server didn't offer to resolve the problem at all. We had to ask for the manager! Our server wasn't proactive, she wasn't empathetic, and she tried to use a "diversion" tactic by trying to divert our attention to dessert instead of the problem we presented to her. **Pathetic**.

Obstacle #5 – The manager's solution was an almost-insulting Coupon for the next visit! **Horrible**.

Why is this important?
Well, have you heard of the word "**Recompense**"?

It's a word you and I rarely hear these days.

It's dictionary-defined as giving someone some type of payment or compensation for loss, damage or injury.

The manager of this steakhouse obviously <u>didn't</u> practice "**Recompense**", <u>and</u> she didn't know about my Secret Formula.

But you will.

I'll be giving you this Secret Formula in another chapter.

If she only knew, the last part of **that** formula would <u>help her make a small short-term "investment" for our guaranteed long-term business as loyal customers.</u>

Had she known the Secret Formula, then she would know that this kind of distasteful food and paltry coupon offer was the tipping point to cause us to **never** want to eat at this restaurant again.

Ever.

Had she known the Formula, she would be well aware that <u>customers have choices</u> and in the future, they would choose a completely different steakhouse which would <u>not allow a customer to leave hungry and unhappy.</u>

They would've valued our business and the potential referrals that we would've given them.

The End Result

Well, sad to say, this is what we actually ended up doing…we have **never returned** to that location nor to any of the other locations of this steakhouse franchise.

My Husband and I have now frequented other steakhouses even though they are much farther from where we live.

When a customer has experienced **several obstacles to having a positive relationship with a company**, that client can feel unhappy, dissatisfied, disgruntled, frustrated, and even angry.

And if that company doesn't promptly respond or worse, doesn't do anything to build that bridge of relationship and trust, **the result will be another lost customer or client.**

When a customer, subscriber, member or patron has experienced several obstacles to having a positive relationship with a company, that client can feel unhappy, dissatisfied, disgruntled, frustrated, and even angry.

If that company doesn't promptly respond or worse, doesn't do anything to build that bridge of relationship and trust, the result will be another lost customer.

This is simply inexcusable.

And easily preventable.

The 4 Takeaways from my Steakhouse Story

As promised, here are 4 Key Takeaways from this true story.

1. Satisfied customers can easily turn into angry or very disgruntled customers.

2. Angry or very disgruntled customers can easily turn into **former customers**.

3. Former customers can easily create other former customers. (Just to be clear, my Husband and I have never steered anyone away from this steakhouse. We've just **never recommended** it. We've also **not** written any negative online reviews about this place. That's just not who we are. All I'm saying is that this is a very real possibility. That former customers can easily create other former customers.)

4. All of this kind of damage can easily been avoided, if you know what to do, when and how.

What Is Customer Loyalty?

L oyal is dictionary-defined as "having or showing complete and constant support for someone or something. Unswerving in allegiance. Faithful or dedicated to someone."

Here are my definitions of a Loyal Customer and Customer Loyalty.

A loyal customer is someone who **loves** availing of the products or services you provide because they <u>consistently feel</u> **great** about their experiences with your company.

They are LOYAL because your service is exceptional. They are loyal because they perceive that whatever they receive from you is at least DOUBLE if not more than the price they pay.

And whatever challenges arise, they know you'll exceed their expectations in how you solve or take care of the problem.

They're dedicated and devoted to you, they'll even rave about you, & actively refer their friends, colleagues, and relatives to you.

And if this is your company culture, these loyal Customers will likely become your lifetime customers.

Customer Loyalty is the **ultimate reward** a company, small business, restaurant or practice receives from their clients when the company consistently provides above average services &/or products, and knows how to resolve problems or issues exceptionally well, and better than their competitors.

Customer Satisfaction vs. Customer Loyalty

I promised to share some of the differences between Customer Satisfaction and Customer Loyalty and why this is a BIG Deal. So let's dive in.

Loyal Customers	Satisfied Customers
Loyal Customers will go through great lengths, even travel farther just to get to you, even if your competitors are closer to where they live or work.	Satisfied Customers are NOT necessarily repeat Customers and may switch to a competitor who is nearer to where they live or work.
Loyal Customers will return to your company over and over again. They are willing to spend more with your company and so in the long run, will bring in more revenue. Why? Because of your excellent product, memorable service, great delivery, and the wonderful experience they consistently get.	Satisfied Customers will shop around or price compare online and even switch to a competitor with a lower or comparable price if they perceive they can get a better value from your competitor.
Loyal Customers will rave about you and refer their friends, colleagues, neighbors and family to you because they trust YOU and LOVE doing business with you. And you'll have the distinct advantage of using the most powerful marketing strategy in the world which doesn't cost you any extra marketing $$ – word-of-mouth advertising.	Satisfied Customers won't necessarily think about you after they purchase from you or avail of your services.

Big Aha!

Here's a BIG Aha for you…Customer Satisfaction is no longer enough.

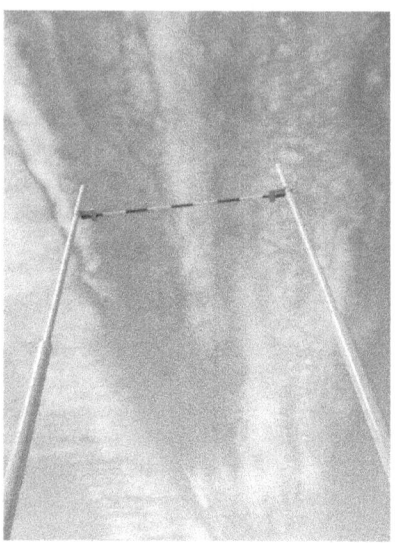

Customer Loyalty is the new "HIGH BAR" to strive for. Customer Satisfaction could very well be at an all-time high, but Customer Loyalty is at an all-time **low**.

And before I show you why, think about my Steakhouse story and the terrible experience I had.

What could the server or the manager have done to ensure that we would be repeat customers?

_____

_____

_____

Think about it.

Then jot down your ideas in the space above.

Well, here are a few of my ideas:

1. The server could have apologized <u>profusely</u> and then offered me dessert on-the-house…**free**.

2. Better yet, the server could have apologized, and then offered <u>both</u> my Husband and me **free** desserts.

3. Either the server or manager could have apologized for the double-wrong that their steak house "served up" for us that night, and then asked the chef to cook up another steak for me. We would've gladly paid for that one. But we were very disgruntled and <u>opposed to paying for a totally burnt, inedible steak.</u>

4. Either the server or the manager could have apologized, then asked the chef to cook up another steak, this time done right, and <u>then not charge us</u> for either the burnt steak or even the newly-cooked one. Ahhh. Now this solution tops them all.

If the steak house had done any of these, especially the last one, do you think we'd come back and perhaps become loyal customers?

You better believe it.

But now, we're not going back….**ever**.

You might be wondering if I'm a loyal customer to anyone. Yes, I'm actually a loyal customer to Amazon.com, Staples – the Office supply store, a handful of restaurants, our Accountant, and my current Dentist.

Your Company's Top Goals Regarding Your Customers

C an you guess what Customer surveys typically ask about? Yes, they ask you to rate their service <u>based on Satisfaction</u>.

Here's a game-changer. One of Your Company's Top Goals needs to be <u>Customer Loyalty</u>. Not merely Customer Satisfaction.

> *One of your company's top goals for as many customers as possible, needs to be Customer Loyalty. Not merely Customer Satisfaction.*

7 Compelling Benefits You'll Get When You Cultivate Customer Loyalty

Now let's talk about 7 Compelling Benefits of Having Loyal Customers.
We'll just breeze through these because they are pretty self-explanatory and I value your time.

When you aim for Customer Loyalty, here are some of the benefits you'll experience…

Compelling Benefit 1

You'll **grow your circle** of Loyal Customers and Raving Fans who will **actively promote** your business. They'll refer their family members, friends, and colleagues to you.

Compelling Benefit 2

You'll consistently increase your business without any additional marketing expense. Yes, zero. How? Through word-of-mouth advertising, of course!

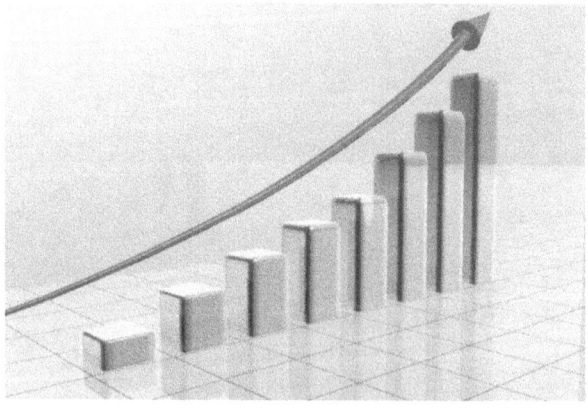

Compelling Benefit 3

You'll Create Brand loyalty.

Your loyal Customers <u>won't even think of going elsewhere</u> because they **love** doing business with your company, they **trust** your team members, and they thoroughly **enjoy** how you and your team make them feel…at <u>every connection point</u>.

Do you have your own favorite brands?

These could be products that you buy often…or services you avail of regularly.

From the car brand you like, to your coffee shop of choice, from your laptop to your phone, your real estate professional to your clothes, you have brand loyalty to at least some or all of these products or services.

Because you want to have recurring streams of revenue, one of your goals is to develop loyalty towards your brand from your customers, clients, members, or subscribers.

Compelling Benefit 4

You and your staff will gain incredible peace of mind knowing that your entire team can handle any and every kind of Customer-related request or issue.

At the very least, you'll lower your stress levels when you eliminate the unnecessary **stress caused by negative online reviews**.

Compelling Benefit 5

You'll keep your solid reputation, and safeguard the good name you've worked hard for years, to uphold.

Compelling Benefit 6

You'll boost employee morale as your staff resolves customer issues with confidence and glowing, positive results.

Compelling Benefit 7

You'll catapult ahead of your competition and propel your business or your practice to greater Success.

Wouldn't you agree that these are incredibly compelling benefits to consider when you look at <u>where your business is</u> regarding the cultivation of Customer Loyalty, and <u>where you could be?</u>

These benefits may seem intangible to you…but I guarantee you that these all affect <u>your bottom line</u>.

Three Lost Keys

3 Lost Keys

Well, we're now at my favorite and most exciting part of this book because I'm going to GIVE you the 3 Lost Keys.

These are Keys your company must acquire and use, in order to develop Customer Loyalty.

When I say lost, I mean that many companies may know about and have heard about these keys.

But they fail to consistently USE these keys.

They fail to train their team, and new team members to use these keys and so these keys are <u>forgotten</u> and eventually LOST by most everyone in the company.

Treasure Chest

A nd because these keys have been lost, many companies lose their opportunity to unlock all the gold that can be found in this treasure chest called Customer Loyalty.

Key #1 – I'll Give You Some Clues…Can You Guess What the Key Is?

I'm very excited about giving you KEY #1.

In fact, I believe this 1ST Key is like a Locksmith's Master Key of All Keys.

It is such a powerful tool that if you only have time to thoroughly master One KEY first, this would be it.

Let's see if you can guess what it is.

It's a **5-letter** word and I'll give you one letter at a time in random order while I quickly explain this key.

Here's the first letter, which is the last letter of the word.

 R

Now I've researched quite a bit, read books, and attended conferences on Customer Service & Customer Loyalty. I've been in the trenches, I've been on the frontlines.

While I was in the Petrochemical industry, I easily developed long-lasting business relationships with customers and vendors from all over the U.S., the U.K., Japan, Thailand, and Mexico because of this KEY.

In the Telecommunications industry, I was able to cultivate numerous trust-based relationships such that I negotiated hundreds of win-win business transactions <u>because of this KEY</u>.

In the Healthcare industry, <u>this KEY helped me tremendously</u> when I interacted face-to-face with 25-30 patients every single day for 8 years from different age groups and all types of socio-economic backgrounds.

Just in this last industry alone, that's easily over 53,000 in-person customer interactions, and **well over half a million phone conversations** during that time span.

Here's the next letter.

H _ _ _ R

In all my years interacting with Customers, Customers and Business Clients, I studied, trained in, and practiced this **BIG FOUNDATIONAL Master Key** in developing Customer Loyalty.

You know what's interesting? **<u>Not one</u>** of the Conference speakers I'd listened to, not one of the books I'd read, not one of the case studies I'd researched ever taught, let alone emphasized this ONE Success Key. Sure, they talk about some of its components…but **not** this word.

And that's just it!

Unfortunately, this key has been virtually lost in our society as a whole, and yet, when we see it demonstrated or displayed in movies, it has the power to move us to tears.

OK, I hope you can guess the word after this letter…

H _ N _ R

Here's the advantage to YOU.

Since this is becoming more uncommon, IF you and your company practice and master this lost key, you will quickly and easily catapult farther ahead of your competition!

And your customers will not only be satisfied...they will be well on their way to becoming **your** loyal customers.

What is this Success Key? The 1ST Lost Key is

H O N O R

You may be wondering, "What in the world is honor? And what does it have to do with Customer Loyalty?" You might even think, "What's the big deal?"

Ahhhh, but it **is** a **big deal**. And we must never underestimate its power.

The Importance of Honor – The Reason Why Millions of $$$ in Customer Service and Phone Skills Training Haven't Worked

Honor is one of the most important things in business.

More specific to our topic, **the utter lack of honor**, is the very reason why Millions of $$$ in Customer Service and Phone Skills Training have **not** worked!

If you "use" and keep using this key called Honor, it will open doors of favor with people for you!

Once you learn this, once you practice this, once you have this KEY in your backpack, <u>you will be unstoppable when it comes to building a growing circle of Loyal Customers and Raving Fans.</u>

And here's why. I'll let you in on another SECRET…

If your company has clients who are from all types of socio-economic and ethnic backgrounds and you're wondering how to relate to such a vast variety of people, you're unclear about how to build rapport, how to serve and how to influence each of them into becoming Loyal Customers or Raving Fans, simply start with this Master Key called HONOR.

Let me explain further.

Begin with a mindset and heart-posture of **HONOR** and begin using **HONORING** language and you will be well on your way. (No not ornery…but **honoring** language.)

Remember this: Honoring Language is acceptable in ANY culture the world over. That bears repeating. Honoring Language is acceptable in ANY culture.

You and your staff can be trained in Customer Service, Phone Skills, and Negotiation techniques.

But when push comes to shove, if a team member doesn't have a <u>core posture of HONOR,</u> all the hours spent on training and all the $$$ spent on conferences are flushed down the toilet.

Well, I'll quickly give you the <u>3 most important components of this Master Key called Honor.</u>

Here they are: **Respect, Integrity and Gratitude**.

You and your staff can be trained in excellent Customer Service, Phone Skills, and Negotiation techniques. But when push comes to shove, if a team member doesn't have a core posture of HONOR, all the hours spent on training and all the $$$ spent on conferences and courses are flushed down the toilet.

Respect

Let's talk about Respect.

Respect means valuing each person.

It means treating each client or customer with dignity, valuing who they are, knowing them by name, accepting them and making sure they feel significant at every connection point with your company.

It means valuing their time, valuing their efforts, and valuing their business.

Did the steakhouse staff **value** our time and our business?

Their actions spoke louder than words. They obviously didn't.

At the Starbucks down the road, they practice **Hospitality** and **Respect**.

They give away free samples of coffee, muffins and other items. That's definitely **Hospitality**.

They value my business, they know me by name and they know what I usually get when I visit them – a Spinach & Feta Breakfast wrap.

That's **Respect**.

Let me go just a bit deeper.

Have you ever encountered this? I know I have…I've met, and at one company, even worked with some friendly individuals <u>who didn't know how to **honor** people</u>.

Guess what would happen…they would become **too** friendly and in the conversation, disrespect or dishonor our customer.

They would bring up topics in a conversation trying to be friendly, and yet it was an inappropriate time or on occasion, an inappropriate topic.

The topic they brough up was downright disrespectful and the dishonored client would show it on their face.

Don't get me wrong…friendliness is wonderful!

We'll discuss this shortly – it's part of Key #2 – Hospitality.

But friendliness has to be combined with **HONOR**.

Are you catching just how important Honor is?

My Personal "Honor" Takeaways from Texas and Japan

I lived in Texas for 18 years and one of the things I learned was that people would say, "Yes, Sir" or "Yes, Ma'am" when addressing others, especially those older than them.

I'm not saying that you should do this.

All I'm saying is that I would rather err on the side of respect & use Sir or Ma'am, Mr. Jones or Mrs. Smith, than addressing them by their first name, especially when they're older than me, and then cause them to feel disrespected.

They can always say, "Oh, just call me Mark" or "You can call me Linda" if they wanted me to address them more informally. And I've had this happen.

When I worked for a Japanese company based in the U.S., I enrolled in Nihongo (Japanese language) classes for a little over a year. As part of those lessons, I also learned the bowing protocol.

So whenever I visited Japan, I would at least know how to converse a little bit with our Japanese colleagues, know how to address and be **respectful** to those who were seniors on the corporate ladder, and also be able to call from the U.S. and get to the right person with ease.

One more important point before we move on.

Respect also includes listening accurately and truly understanding your customers' needs and desires, and regularly and dependably delivering to these needs.

It also means being adaptable to your Customers' changing needs as well.

Integrity

The 2ND component of Honor is Integrity. Integrity means Honesty and Trustworthiness.

It means that because I want to honor someone, I keep my word.

When I promise a customer that I'll call them back at a certain time, I do. And just in case I'm unable to, I contact them as soon as I'm able and sincerely apologize to them.

When I was in the oil and gas industry, I had a handful of shipments over the years that were going to be delayed by several days. As soon as I'd find out about these delays, I'd called my customers right away, inform them about the situation and ask if this would be a problem. If it was, I'd offer solutions.

Integrity means being early or on time for appointments, keeping promises, being ethical, being someone they can trust, and being honest with them about what's *really* going on instead of hiding things that they should know about.

Gratitude

The 3RD component of Honor is Gratitude. When you honor someone, it means being thankful for that person.

In wedding invitations, you usually see this phrase: we request the **honor** of your presence. It means, they would be so grateful if you could attend the wedding and celebrate with them.

So when it comes to guests at our company, it means being grateful for these clients and thankful for our customers.

Here's something that has helped me practice Gratitude every day.

I have a journal that I carry with me and first thing in the morning, as soon as I get up, during my time of meditation, I list down at least 1 thing I'm grateful for.

Whether it's being grateful for a team member who provided me with crucial information in a timely manner, or my Husband who prepared a delicious cup of hot chocolate for me, being thankful for any and every bit of progress our children make, or a solution to a problem I was able to solve, or having gratitude for a client who sent me and my team a thank you card. I jot at least a couple of things and glance at them during the day.

So when challenges arise, I am able to have a heart-posture of Honor and a mindset of Gratitude.

It helps put me in a place wherein I don't feel like I'm a victim of situations or of people. I am able to view challenging circumstances and even demanding people with a positive attitude and a mindset of abundance.

The bottom line is that Honor – with its 3 KEY components of Respect, Integrity and Gratitude will give YOU an unfair advantage over your competition in developing Customer Loyalty.

Actionable Idea

Try this for the next 30 days

Write down at least one person you're grateful for either, on your journal or on a calendar you have and use all the time.

And write down one reason you're grateful for that person. Now glance at what you wrote once or twice during course of the day.

See if this helps you develop a posture of Honor and Gratitude toward people.

Key# 2 – Hospitality

The second Lost Key is Hospitality. Let me explain what it means in the business world, and why I believe it is one of the 3 Lost Keys.

Hospitality

Here's my definition of hospitality. It means being…

- Welcoming

- Generous

- Friendly

- and in the proper context, FUN

A famous Hebrew scholar once wrote, "Always be eager to practice hospitality."

It's sad, but there are many, businesses, stores, legal, financial or healthcare practices and companies whose employees are <u>anything but</u> welcoming and friendly.

It's as though they hailed from **I'm-too-busy-for-you-so-don't-bother-me Grump Town**.

You know what I LOVE to do when I encounter people from Grump Town?

I make it my personal challenge to get them out of Grump mode, to engage in light and friendly banter and at the <u>very least</u> to make them **smile**!

And what motivates me to keep doing this is that, in all humility, my batting average is in the high 900's. ☺

Hospitality – Let's Get Practical

Here's something to mull over -- According to the dictionary, "Hospitality" is also the activity of **providing food, drinks**, etc. <u>for people who are the guests or customers of an organization.</u> Hmmm…interesting, huh?

Well, if you think about it, isn't it refreshing to be a customer of a business whose employees greet you, smile and are friendly toward you? And wouldn't it be amazing **if** they even offered you a beverage?

If you've ever visited a Lexus dealership, you'll know what I'm talking about. Oh yes. They practice exceptional Hospitality, even if you're <u>not</u> the person who's buying the car.

Now I'm **not** suggesting that you purchase a $3,000 coffee maker and hire a barista to serve every customer that comes in.

All I'm recommending is that you brainstorm a couple more ways you can implement being **more** hospitable, welcoming, and generous to your customers, than you already are at the moment.

Well, this very important key has been forgotten, lost in a number of companies.

And remember, Hospitality is not just for the Hospitality industry like hotels, resorts and restaurants. No! It's for every company, every business, and every practice.

Have you ever considered having a hot beverage or a cold drink of water available to your customers?

When my Husband and I invite guests over to our home, we do our best to practice hospitality. We have a Welcome mat at our front door.

We **welcome** our visitors by greeting them with open arms, warm smiles and we make them feel at home. We prepare more than enough food and drink, and express our **generosity** toward them.

What we want most is for them to have the most enjoyable and fun time at our home. Wouldn't you do the same? Of course you would.

Well, this same experience needs to be what your customers experience at your practice, at your office, **and** <u>at every connection point</u>.

By phone, email, snail mail letters, face-to-face conversations and online interactions.

Success Tip

Here's a helpful TIP: Start viewing your clients or customers as – **your guests**. Yes, your guests. Yet what do most companies have right by their door…a welcome mat? Guess again.

They have at least one "No Soliciting" sign!

Do you think these signs ever stop solicitors? No!

So what's the point of making 99% of the people that walk through your doors – your customers -- feel a bit unwelcome by that "No Soliciting" sign?

When your team begins viewing and truly treating your Customers as Guests, it may seem like a slight change in mindset to you.

But the way your team will engage, converse and serve Guests will be light years ahead of your competitor who treats their Clients as unwelcome interruptions.

Friendly

Let's talk about the word Friendly.

Jeffrey Gitomer – an American author, professional speaker, and business trainer – says,

"If there are 100 qualities of a successful customer service person or salesperson – friendly is in the top three, and may be the top one."

Where Are You on the Friendly Scale

Allow me to ask you. Are you friendly? Is your staff friendly? On a scale of 1 to 10, how friendly are you?

If you and your staff are a consistent 9 or a 10, then your likelihood of developing Loyal Customers is extremely high. Congratulations!

Now if you have a grump or a couple of them who work at your company, legal or financial practice, or in your business, **train** them in <u>consistent</u> Friendliness and Hospitality.

And if you've done everything you could possibly do to help them, & all else fails, move them elsewhere and replace them with happy and friendly people.

Actionable Ideas

Try ANY one of these Action Points for this Key called Hospitality.

1. Replace any "No Soliciting" sign with a Welcome mat or a Welcome sign.

2. If a grumpy-looking customer or client comes to your office, make it your personal challenge to get them to smile before they leave.

3. Get the book "How to Win Friends and Influence People" by Dale Carnegie and read a page or 2-a-day before you start work. And not on company time. ☺

I invite you to visit www.JackieMorey.com & register for your FREE Customer Loyalty Boot Camp video course ($127 value).

Key #3 – Topnotch, Creative Problem-solving

Well, I hope you're thoroughly enjoying this book. Here's the 3RD and final key that I promised to share with you.

Key #3 is Topnotch, Creative Problem-solving.

Problems

Let's face it. We live in an imperfect world and mistakes will be made, shipments will be delayed, steaks will be burned, products will have defects, and problems will come up.

This Key is absolutely vital to developing Customer Loyalty because **how** you handle problems when they arise will determine whether you'll lose a customer to your competitors **or** have a devoted and loyal customer.

I'm going to give you 2 components of this crucial KEY.

I also invite you to please visit www.JackieMorey.com to get more information about this very important topic.

The first component is a mindset that **everyone** who wants to gain this skill of topnotch, creative problem-solving needs to have.

The second component is my proven Secret Formula that has worked over and over again in overcoming problems and developing loyal customers.

Proactive

Ok, here we go. The very first component is having a Proactive, winning mindset regarding problems.

For me personally, the word "Proactive" means a couple of things. It means...

1. Taking ownership of a problem instead of finding blaming. It means "owning the problem" and helping the customer or at least reassuring the customer that you will help them by finding a solution.

2. Being willing to take action towards finding a solution rather than waiting for someone else to solve the problem.

Without a proactive mindset, you'll be coming from a position of scarcity instead of a **posture of abundance**. So this component is incredibly important.

L.E.A.R.N.

Let's go to the 2ND component.

I will now reveal MY Secret Formula for Topnotch, Creative Problem-solving. It's a winning strategy that I've personally come up with and use all the time.

It's something that no one else teaches and I'm giving it away to you practically FREE.

Oh, and by the way, it's the formula that I wish the Steak house manager had known when we visited her restaurant that night.

The formula is L.E.A.R.N.

L is for Listen

E is for Empathize

A is for Apologize

R is for Resolve the Problem

N is for Now Wow & Delight your customer

Let's go through this briefly. The first four – Listen, Empathize, Apologize and Resolve the Problem are very important, but let's focus on the last letter "N".

I have some very important Tips and Strategies regarding these first 4 so please check out www.JackieMorey.com for details.

The last one -- **Now Wow and Delight your Customer** is what I'd like to discuss with the time we have left.

After we've listened, empathized, apologized, resolved a problem, we're not done.

Going back to my Steakhouse story, neither our Server nor the Manager resolved the problem.

There was no recompense for the burnt steak they served me, nor the very long wait times we had to put up with.

There was no apology for the horrible experience at their restaurant.

And the paltry coupon given by the manager certainly didn't Wow nor Delight me.

Now Wow and Delight your customer means going above and beyond resolving the problem, to ensuring that in the customer's mind, they won't even hesitate continuing to do business with you.

Instead, they'll feel **great** about going back to your company, availing of your products and services, returning over and over again to your practice or business, and in the near future, referring their friends and family to you.

Now Wow and Delight – Real Stories

A Staples Story You Can Glean From

I'll give you a couple of examples to demonstrate this Secret Sauce.

One day, I went to Staples – an office supply chain - to have a 500-page pdf file, printed on copy paper. They said there were a few jobs ahead of mine, so it would take a couple of hours.

No problem. I could leave and then come back in 2 hours. I was heading to the library, anyway, and I could easily fill that time with reading and writing.

When I returned 2-1/2 hours later, the lady who helped me had already gone home.

The new person at their Print and Copy Center told me that the job hadn't even been started.

She immediately **apologized profusely** and explained that they had one huge copy machine down and it had been down since the previous day.

She also informed me that they had already placed a call the previous day for the Service Guy to come out and repair it, but he hadn't shown up since then.

In the meantime, she said she'd start my order **right away** and it would take 30 minutes.

I really needed this project done that day, so I told her I'd come back in 30 minutes.

When I returned, she showed me that it was almost done and started putting a huge chunk of the copied pages inside a portable box.

After 7 more minutes, the job was done.

She had a couple of other customers in line. Not a problem. She didn't allow this to faze here.

She acknowledged them and informed them that she'd be right back, as she walked with me to the nearby check-out counter.

On the way, she explained to me that she would give me a discount.

When we got to the register, she told the cashier to give me **50% off of my order** which was originally a little under $100. I ended up paying ONLY about $45! Wow...I was delighted!

This is how topnotch, creative problem-solving looks like.

Now, I'm happy to report that I'm a loyal customer of Staples.

One Phone Conversation with Mary Saved the Day

Here's my final example. I've modified some of the details for confidentiality purposes.

When I worked in the Healthcare industry, we had a customer, let's call her Mary, who needed a very important cardiac test done at our office.

Mary had called to cancel her test which was coming up in 2

days.

It was a long, 4-hour test and we had scheduled seven (7) other customers for that day and had hired a topnotch technician to perform this test for our customers.

A member of our team explained to me that we had a problem. We needed at least eight (8) customers in order to cover our overhead costs such as hiring the top-level technician, and for us to make a small profit.

So it was important for Mary to proceed with the test.

The team member told me that Mary knew she needed the test, but couldn't afford the test and she supposedly didn't feel comfortable with how long it would take – 4 hours.

I was given this problem to solve. Why? Because I had become known in our office as a Problem Solver, a Solution Provider.

I knew Mary and she knew me well. I had built rapport with her in the few months we knew each other by being hospitable, friendly and by showing honor and respect toward her.

Before I called her up, I did my research on her health insurance. I knew our fixed cost for the test, and based on her insurance plan, I calculated the flexibility margin and still make a little bit of profit.

When I got in touch with Mary, I **listened** to her explain her concerns & I **empathized** with her.

She expressed that she <u>knew</u> she needed this important test…she knew it was medically necessary.

Now here's the mind-blowing importance of listening **and** empathizing.

I found out as I focused in on Mary's needs and wants, that it <u>wasn't</u> so much the length of the test that was her main concern and causing her to want to cancel. No.

It was because she got confused by all the preparations for the test, she also felt pressured by one of our team members, AND yes, she also admitted that she didn't have the money that week to pay for her customer portion of the test, the portion which her insurance wouldn't cover.

So here's what I did.

First, I sincerely **apologized** for the way one of our team members had confused her and caused her to feel pressured.

Next, I began to **resolve** and **"Now Wow and Delight"** her. I promptly addressed her money concerns.

I explained to her how much her insurance was actually going to cover, how much her customer portion was, then I offered her a discount.

She felt relieved and was quite pleased with the discount.

Then I asked her, "Mary, what if I not only offered you this discount, but I'm also willing to divide up the total, and spread it out into 3 payments instead of one lump sum, and with Zero interest charges?"

She said, "Really? Oh, I could definitely do that! That would work with my budget!"

I could tell over the phone that she was really happy about this.

It was a win-win situation. She said, she'd keep her scheduled exam and asked me to help her understand the preparations. I gladly and painstakingly explained the preparation, step-by-step.

Not only that. I even addressed any concerns with how long the test was.

I said that we had several different magazines and books at our office, but invited her to bring her favorite books, magazines and, because I knew she LOVED to knit, she could bring her knitting materials.

I believe that I had wowed and delighted her because by the end of our conversation, (you know how you can tell when someone is smiling on the other end of the phone), well, she was beaming, and told me she was looking forward to a few hours of knitting.

She thanked me a LOT. And when I saw her come in for her cardiac test, she thanked me over and over again.

That's an example of Problem Solving that will really help develop Customer Loyalty.

Actionable Idea

Think of a problem you or your company experienced recently that wasn't resolved to the customer's satisfaction.

What could have been done **not only to resolve the issue**, but to "Now Wow and Delight Your Customer"?

This is one of the most overlooked and yet vital Actionable Ideas in this book.

Brainstorm some ideas with your team and come up with at least 3 ways to "Now Wow and Delight Your Customers."

Promise delivered.

Well, there you go.

We've covered the definition of Customer Loyalty, we've seen some of the differences between Customer Satisfaction and Customer Loyalty, we also discussed The 7 Compelling Benefits You'll Get when you Focus on Cultivating Customer Loyalty, & not merely Customer Satisfaction.

And finally, I gave you 3 Lost Keys your company can now use to your advantage in order to cultivate Customer Loyalty and thrive in a challenging economy.

I've also given you several Actionable Ideas that you can implement right away so that you can begin developing a company culture that values and consistently aims for Customer Loyalty.

I'm Jackie Morey. It's been an honor to share with you today. Thank you so much for being my Customer. I value you, and your time. I look forward to connecting with you soon. ☺

What's Next?

Thank you for reading…I hope you enjoyed this book! I also hope I've been able to bring lots of value to you and have helped you.

Here's what I'd like to recommend that you do next. Just 3 simple things:

1. I encourage you to try one or more of the Actionable Ideas we talked about in this book.

2. I invite you to please visit www.JackieMorey.com and get your FREE Customer Loyalty Boot Camp video course ($127 value) with more Game-changing Customer Loyalty Strategies and Cutting-edge Marketing solutions.

3. Keep an eye out for upcoming books, webinars and online training courses that my Husband – Jim and I are cooking up for you. Our goal is to provide you with at least 2X, and up to 10X the value of what any of our customers invest in our products and services. Please check out www.CustomerStrategyAcademy.com.

Here's a preview:

"Every professional practice or small business needs a blueprint or a system to develop Customer Loyalty, because we now live in a world where your customers can comparison shop, or view your online reputation in seconds on their mobile device." ~Jackie Morey

What Others are Saying about Jackie

"There are many who teach Customer Service and a few who teach Customer Loyalty. But if you want to reach World-Class level, Jackie Morey helps you get there."

– Brian Bosché, Founder & CEO of BeReadyMEDIA.com - Powerhouse Media Consulting

"Jackie's considerable customer service experience combined with her professionalism and commitment to excellence make her an excellent choice if you are interested in moving your company to the next level in Customer Satisfaction. Her integrity and attention to detail will earn your trust. What she can do for your company will earn your respect and appreciation."

– Michael Hartsfield, President of Aileron Private Client Services

"Jackie is a powerful customer acquisition force with both her extensive knowledge and her effective implementation tactics. I love working with Jackie because she pinpoints the weak points in my Customer Strategy while offering the perfect solutions. Every business would benefit from a thorough Jackie Customer-Strategy audit."

– Bridgette Hart, CEO of InHouse HR and Hart Connections

"Jackie is a creative business thinker and entrepreneur. Her broad experience makes her well-suited as a leader, designer and Idea Developer. If you need top notch C-level help, Jackie is your gal."

– Greg Linnebach, Business Development Executive at TIR, International

"Jackie Morey is an entrepreneur, excellent in areas of team building, problem solving, strategy, managing and coaching large and small groups."

– Judy Reynolds, Program Coordinator at Leadership Thurston County, former Executive Director at Future Business Leaders of America, Washington State

"If you or your staff are experiencing problems with challenging Customer issues, look no further! Jackie Morey's expertise in training small businesses, medical practices and larger organizations to successfully deal with these concerns is incomparable."

– Pamela Pollock, MBA, CPC, MA, Entrepreneur and Owner of "Pamela Pollock, LLC" a counseling and coaching practice in Seattle, WA.

"Jackie is a premier problem-solver and trainer in her field, producing unequaled customer service results. Descriptions such as, "Integrous, effective communicator, attention to detail and follow-through," come to mind in describing Jackie Morey."

– Dayna Belcher, Founder of Transformed Living

Jackie's Bio

Jackie Morey is a nationally recognized Customer Loyalty Strategist, Co-Founder and COO of Customer Strategy Academy.

She has literally helped thousands of customers, entrepreneurs, service professionals, executives, and companies both nationally and internationally from all ages, and a wide variety of socio-economic and ethnic backgrounds

Jackie has over 29 years of experience serving clients from Microsoft, Boeing, Amazon.com, Deloitte, other Fortune 500 companies, as well as small to medium business owners, financial professionals, legal firms and healthcare companies.

She helps them achieve success in

- Creating Raving Fans

- Achieving Win-Win through Stress-free Negotiation

- Sales and Marketing

- Team Building

- Revenue Collection and so much more

Happily married to her husband Jim, they have a son and a daughter who "make them proud" every day. They live in a beautiful Pacific Northwest suburb of Seattle.

Hi, I'm Jackie Morey.

I honor, encourage, appreciate and give value first.

I see the best in people, celebrate their uniqueness, and enjoy serving and helping them succeed to their highest capabilities and to peak levels.

I do my best to be the best at what I love to do.

I love inspiring, encouraging, supporting, serving and coaching people.

I invite you to connect with me! I'm on…

LinkedIn: www.LinkedIn.com/in/JackieMorey1

Twitter: @JackieMorey1

Web: www.JackieMorey.com

Web: www.CustomerStrategyAcademy.com

Book Photo Credits in Order of Appearance

1. © Wavebreakmedia at Depositphotos.com
2. © Wavebreakmedia at Depositphotos.com
3. © paulfleet at Depositphotos.com
4. Courtesy of "Jeff Bezos' iconic laugh" by Steve Jurvetson - Flickr: Bezos' Iconic Laugh. Licensed under CC BY 2.0 via Commons - https://commons.wikimedia.org/wiki/File:Jeff_Bezos%27_iconic_laugh.jpg#/media/File:Jeff_Bezos%27_iconic_laugh.jpg
5. © bizoon at Depositphotos.com
6. © resnick_joshua1 at DepositPhotos.com
7. © kosmos111 at Depositphotos.com
8. © ajafoto at Depositphotos.com
9. © depositedhar at Depositphotos.com
10. © wukasa at Depositphotos.com
11. © vmaarbess at Depositphotos.com
12. © Amitofo at Depositphotos.com
13. © Wavebreakmedia at Depositphotos.com
14. © Almagami at Depositphotos.com
15. © Feedough and Wavebreakmedia respectively at Depositphotos.com
16. © Donets at Depositphotos.com
17. © Andresr at Depositphotos.com
18. © pressmaster at Depositphotos.com
19. © Wavebreakmedia at Depositphotos.com
20. © ThomasAmby at Depositphotos.com
21. © Wavebreakmedia at Depositphotos.com
22. © chrisdorney at Depositphotos.com
23. © urbanbuzz at Depositphotos.com
24. © Rawpixel at Depositphotos.com
25. © donscarpo at Depositphotos.com
26. © icetray at Depositphotos.com
27. © Wavebreakmedia at Depositphotos.com
28. © monticello at Depositphotos.com
29. © wabeno at Depositphotos.com
30. © kelpfish at Depositphotos.com
31. © iofoto at Depositphotos.com
32. courtesy of Jeffrey Gitomer
33. © andresr and Wavebreakmedia respectively at Depositphotos.com
34. © stokette, cybernesco and Maridav respectively at Depositphotos.com
35. © stuartmiles at Depositphotos.com
36. © M_Prusaczyk at Depositphotos.com
37. StaplesHwy7-3.jpg. From Wikimedia Commons, the free media repository
38. © racorn at Depositphotos.com
39. © racorn at Depositphotos.com

www.ingramcontent.com/pod-product-compliance
Lightning Source LLC
Chambersburg PA
CBHW070841180526
45168CB00002B/919